Eyles Irwin

Occasional Epistles Written During a Journey from London to

Busrah

In the Gulf of Persia, in the years 1780 and 1781 : to William Hayley

Eyles Irwin

Occasional Epistles Written During aJourney from London to Busrah
In the Gulf of Persia, in the years 1780 and 1781 : to William Hayley

ISBN/EAN: 9783744756396

Printed in Europe, USA, Canada, Australia, Japan

Cover: Foto ©Andreas Hilbeck / pixelio.de

More available books at **www.hansebooks.com**

OCCASIONAL EPISTLES.

WRITTEN DURING A

JOURNEY FROM LONDON TO BUSRAH,

IN THE GULF OF PERSIA,

IN THE YEARS 1780 AND 1781.

To WILLIAM HAYLEY, Esq.

By EYLES IRWIN, Esq.

LONDON:
PRINTED FOR J. DODSLEY, IN PALL MALL.

M.DCC.LXXXIII.

E P I S T L E I.

FROM VENICE.

ARGUMENT.

Subject proposed.—Author's address to his friend.—Venice —review of her former greatness, compared to her present insignificancy—her affinity with Rome.—Rivalship of the Roman prowess and moderation.—Eminent men— Morosini—Arrizzo—Marc Antonio Bragadino—Palma. —League of Cambray.—Policy of the senate.—Transition to the probable state of Venice some ages hence.—Gaiety of the Venetians.—Elegant style of buildings.—Palladio— Sansovin.—Museum of Farsetti.—Conclusion.

EPISTLE I.

FROM VENICE.

THE Rhine and Danube pafs'd, the Alps o'ercome,
    Venice furvey'd—and yet the Traveller dumb !
Not light the labor, to a vacant mind,
To fill the fketch which ADDISON defign'd :
Nor will fuccefs more juftify the aim,   5
Tho' friendfhip lean on fome eftablifh'd name.

   Yet, while poetic fcenes my fong invite,
To thee, my HAYLEY, I prefume to write ;
HAYLEY, whofe genius bold on Learning's fhore
Has touch'd, like COOK, where Bard ne'er touch'd before ;
Whofe Mufe, like Pallas from the Thunderer's brain, 11
Iffu'd adult, the faireft of the train.

B 2
B 2   To

To thee I write, whose numbers have portray'd
The art first try'd by Corinth's tender maid ;
From scenes where Titian his soft graces caught,   15
Where Romney studied, and where Paulo taught.

   Late as I stray'd, the healthful breeze to take,
Where proud Ca' Dona overhangs the lake,
From whose clear bosom circling islets rise,
Whose glittering steeples mingle with the skies ;   20
Beyond whose banks extends the fruitful ground,
Which Brenta waters, and the Alps surround ;
Wrapt in the scenes that open'd to my view,
To happier times my busy fancy flew ;
And as the contrast to contempt I gave,   25
Methought a voice low murmur'd from the wave.

   " Venice ! at once thy Genius' pride and shame !
" Degenerate semblance of thy antient fame !
" Where now contend those rivals in the race ?
" Have Arts or Arms priority of place ?   30
" The only vestige of their golden reign
" An useless arsenal or mould'ring fane ;
" Where Titian's tints, Palladian domes decay,
" To time consign'd by sad neglect a prey.

                                                                                        " Nor

" Nor more thy Natives rife in my efteem ;   35
" Peculiar, as thy fite, their manners feem.
" Bred up to forms, effentials they defpife,
" And only mafk'd, when aping to be wife.
" Born of the wave whence amorous Venus came,
" Thy daughters glow with the contagious flame ; 40
" Affert the empire which their beauty gave,
" And bind the lover an eternal flave.
" Hence manly wifdom has abjur'd the ftate,
" Vigor of thought, and freedom of debate :
" Hence warlike cares to ferious trifles yield,   45
" And Venus drives thy Genius from the field :
" Hence, tho' Ambition waits to leap the mound,
" In melting mufic each alarm is drown'd ;
" And hoftile rumors, that from Auftria fly,
" Strike, like the lute, thine ear, and, ftriking, die." 50
    The city's Guardian fpoke her humbled pride,
And ceafing, plung'd beneath the filent tide.
Touch'd at her plaint, I check'd each harfher thought,
And chang'd my tone as truth and pity taught.
    " Not that with jaundic'd, or with Gothic eye, 55
" Thy worth o'erlooking, thy defects I fpy ;

" Not

" Not that, with thought profane, I flight the crown,

" Which Neptune yielded to thy juft renown.

" No—beauteous emprefs of th' Italic main !

" Great was thy caufe, and gallant were thy train.   60

" Drawn here by Freedom from their native land,

" Thine iflands cherifh'd Rome's expiring band ;

" Who, worthy of the fountain whence they fprung,

" Oft on the rear of frighted Othman hung ;

" Till of her turban'd tyrants ridding Greece,   65

" Like Rome, they gave her liberty and peace.

" Great as Æmilius, in that hallow'd hour

" When wond'ring nations bleft the victor's pow'r ;

" When Glory hail'd him at th' Olympic game,

" And refcu'd Freedom twin'd his wreath of fame.   70

  " Thefe were the records of thine earlier days,

" When Arts confpir'd to fpread the hero's praife :

" When to his mem'ry fculptur'd trophies rofe

" To feal his triumphs o'er his country's foes.

" There Palma's pencil for the laurel ftrives,   75

" And Morofini in his art furvives !

" There Time beholds the Candian chief with joy,

" The fiege fuftain which doubled that of Troy :

                                    " Beholds

" Beholds him, happier ftill in manhood's pride,

" Annex Morea to his country's fide.   80

" Arrizzo, glorying in a cruel death,

" In marble here again refigns his breath.

" Sufpended by falfe Muftapha on high,

" Still brave Antonio may his fate defy :

" What tho' his body taint the wholefome gale,   85

" Ne'er fhall thy incenfe, Public Virtue ! fail.

" Yet at his name the Turk aghaft is thrown,

" Nor dares to challenge Cyprus as his own.

" Shades of renown ! and Patriots ever dear !

" Whofe wayward end awakes the foreign tear,   90

" Permit a ftranger, friendly to your fhore,

" T'affay the value of no common ore.

"   " Long prov'd thy ftate a barrier to the Turk,

" And foundeft policy upheld the work.

" Envy to calm, fhe trufted to intrigue,   95

" And, artful, broke the force of Cambray's league.

" This Europe faw, and trembled for her date,

" When priefts and potentates confpir'd her fate.

" But vain thofe fears—to Julius fhe apply'd,

" And fapp'd the mifchief by the Pontiff's pride.   100

" Tho'

" Tho' Venice now with faded fplendor fhine,

" She fhews, like Athens, beauteous in decline :

" And ages hence, when crumbling to a wafte,

" Her ruins fhall attract the eye of Tafte.

" Then, as the traveller roves in thoughtful mood,   105

" Where Marco's tower, or San Benètto ftood,

" Here (fhall he cry) once throng'd the young and gay,

" Here laugh'd and fung, and charm'd their cares away.

" At mafs or play, unmafk'd or mafk'd the fame,

" Love all their motive ! pleafure all their aim !   110

" Yet, in this whirlpool found the Arts a place,

" And temples rofe, which antient Rome might grace,

" Deck'd with the fpoils of many a falling pile,

" That erft o'erlook'd the Bofphorus or Nile :

" Statues, that borrow'd life from Phydias' hand,   115

" And palaces, by chafte Pailadio plann'd :

" Models of tafte ! which Attic palms might win,

" And with Lyfippus clafs a Sanfovin.

" Oft have the curious of a diftant foil,

" Deriv'd new lights from learn'd Farfetti's toil :   120

" Whofe treafures, drawn from mines of claffic earth,

" Befpoke a fpirit noble as his birth.

3   " But

" But humbled now the wonder of her age,

" Sad proof of change, and Time's deftructive rage !

" Bare thefe canals to Alpine breezes lie ; 125

" Where row'd the ftately barge the fifhers ply :

" Once more a village—Venice all deplore—

" She proves what Triefte may be, and Tadmor was

  " before !"

 Purfuits like thefe engage thy abfent friend,

The fenfe they flatter, and the tafte amend. 130

As the bold merchant leaves his native fhore,

The wealth of unknown regions to explore,

The Bard, a bankrupt ! now redeems his time

In culling fubjects from a richer clime,

Subjects untouch'd by wit, and new to rhime. 135

How wide the footing on which Poets ftand,

Whofe fway extends o'er Fancy's magic land !

Who, in their hand if Learning's light expire,

Relume their tapers at Invention's fire.

Lo ! where th'advent'rous train my HAYLEY leads, 140

Tries every courfe, and in each courfe fucceeds :

Ev'n here the precepts of his art prevail,

And with his praifes teems the weftern gale.

    C   Warm'd

Warm'd by the theme, my fpirits mount in flame,
And emulation wakens at the name :   145
An emulation which may Bards impel,
Which loves the merit it would fain excel ;
Which, if it mifs, as now, its daring end,
Still joys to grace the triumph of a friend.

EPISTLE

E P I S T L E II.

FROM LAODICEA.

ARGUMENT.

Voyage from Venice to the coast of Syria—Adriatic Gulf—Coast of Apulia—Epirus—Isle of Corcyra—Coast of Arcadia—Corinth—Mount Parnassus—Cape Methone—Isle of Cytherea—Shores of Sparta—Crete.—Reflexions on the change in the Archipelago.—Islands of Milo—Nio—Paros—Naxos—Cos—Rhodes.—Unpleasing picture of the present state of Greece.—Cyprus—fatal revolution in the climate, soil, government, and population, of this island.—View of the Syrian coast—Mount Lebanon—Cities of Tyre—Scanderoon, Seleucia, Antioch, Laodicea.—Preference due to Britain from a comparison with these countries.—Conclusion.

EPISTLE II.

FROM LAODICEA.

ONCE more the lyre, my Mufe, advent'rous fweep,
   Plac'd on the margin of the Syrian deep :
What lands and feas we pafs'd, the ftrains rehearfe—
Will HAYLEY hear, while Greece adorns the verfe ?

Down Adria's gulf our bark directs her courfe,   5
Storm'd by the wave, and Eurus' wintry force.
What time the antients us'd in port to ftay,
We fteer where on our right Apulia lay ;
And fam'd Epirus' adverfe coaft explore,
Whence Pyrrhus thunder'd on the Roman fhore.   10
Thine ifle, Corcyra ! next attracts our view,
Where wife Ulyffes met a warrior's due ;

Where

Where the tir'd chief a sweet asylum found,
From toils and tempests snatch'd to friendly ground.

   Onward our bark the northern breeze impell'd,   15
Which by Arcadia's coast her voyage held:
That op'ning gulf the narrow isthmus laves,
Where Corinth reign'd the sovereign of the waves.
Parnassus here his forked summit shows;
In lieu of laurels bears eternal snows.   20
Alpheus now, without a fiction, glides,
While not a swan disports upon his tides.
Emblems of change! which Grecia's pride has crost,
Her Freedom fetter'd, and her Genius lost.

   The vernal airs bespeak a softer clime,   25
As we approach the themes of antient time.
Fill'd with the thought, I feel my breast expand,
And anxious double bleak Methone's strand.
The shifting prospects still our hours beguile,
And now we gaze on Cytherea's isle.   30
Birth-place of Venus and of Helen, hail!
Thy praise to reach, what numbers may prevail?—
All hearts acknowledge Cytherea's sway,
And Helen still inflames in Homer's lay.

9   Eastward

Eaftward from hence our profperous courfe we fteer, 35
And with the morn fucceeding lands appear.
Black on our left the hilly regions lour,
Where Spartan virtue held the reins of pow'r:
Or where, in darker times, the fable grew
Of Hydras, Centaurs, which the hero flew.   40
In Lerna's fen, or Pholoe's favage height,
Worfe monfters now the ravag'd land affright;
Nor lives an Hercules, mankind to right!
Thence to the fouth I turn my fearching eyes,
Where, eaftward ftretching, Crete's fteep cliffs arife,   45
With Ida and her hundred cities crown'd,
But more for Minos and his laws renown'd:
Tho' thefe but on hiftoric records ftand,
And thofe, in ruins, ftill denote the land.

What ifles, alternate, on th' horizon crowd—   50
Once feats of freedom, now to bondage bow'd!
O! dire reverfe of ftates and things below,
Nor arts, nor arms, exempt mankind from woe:
Their boafted knowledge but their fall contrives,
And fell defpair their wither'd ftrength furvives.   55
Thus fighs the Mufe in paffing Milo's coaft,
And Nio, proud of Homer's urn to boaft:

Serphos,

Serphos, on which the fabled scene is laid,
Whence Perseus rescu'd the devoted maid :
Paros, whose marble gave the isle to fame ;   60
And Naxos, whence the god of vintage came.
With fonder joy she views the Coan coast,
Where Med'cine's pride arose, and Painting's boast.
Hail, happy land! of living fame secure,
While Genius is esteem'd and Arts endure.   65

    Her northward course our veffel keeps no more,
But steers obliquely to the Rhodian shore,
Where the Coloffus rear'd his tow'ring head,
And where his shatter'd frame the groaning earth o'erspread:
Like him the Turk, too large a realm embrac'd,   70
One foot on Afia, one on Europe plac'd,
Totters at Destiny's destructive call,
And strong convulsions indicate his fall.

    Yet still fair Grecia bends beneath his yoke,
Her regions wasted, and her spirit broke :   75
Plenty and Industry forsake her plains,
And Want and Indolence debase her swains.
All! all! her former lustre worn away,
Save still that Beauty gilds her closing day.

                          Heavens !

Heavens! at that name I lose my rising spleen,   80
Lo! we approach the seat of Beauty's Queen.
This day from Rhodes we cleave the Halcyon sea,
Next, fallen Cyprus! gives us sight of thee.
Was't not enough to mourn inteſtine jars,
Drought, famine, ſlavery, peſtilence, and wars!   85
Thy Paphos levell'd, and a waſte thy ſoil,
That now thy daughters prove the tyrant's ſpoil?
Hence population rolls a languid tide,
While Turkiſh walls her injur'd ſources hide.
Bright Goddeſs! thou, aſſert thy ſex's cauſe,   90
And blaſt the rude contemner of thy laws:
By Beauty tended, let him own thy fires,
But chill with ſcorn his arrogant deſires.

　　Soon to the Cyprian ſhore we bid adieu,
And Syria's region riſes to our view.   95
Majeſtic Lebanon his head uprears,
White with the winter of a thouſand years:
Tho' fall'n his pride, ſome cedars yet remain,
Protected ſtill by David's ſacred ſtrain.

Line 9.—The gather'd winter of a thouſand years.   Pope.

D   Hence

Hence to the fouth I look, through fancy's eye,   100
Neglected, fcorn'd !—where Tyre's proud relics lie.
Ah ! haplefs miftrefs of Phenicia's realms,
Thee time affails, and tyranny o'erwhelms.
Thofe walls, which turn'd young Ammon's conqu'ring
      fword,
Yield to each fummons of an Arab horde !   105
That haven, where a navy rode in ftate,
Can fcarcely fhield the fifher from his fate !
Not fo when Dido fled thy hoftile ftrand,
To found a city in a kinder land.
Alas ! we blindly reafon's impulfe try,   110
And Tyre and Carthage but in ruin vie !
   Now northward bound, the bark her helm obeys—
A fudden calm her rapid progrefs ftays.
Inactive held, we view the diftant fhore,
Which takes new forms and changes tints no more.   115
Stretch'd in a line, we pierce its utmoft bound,
Where moift, unpeopled Scanderoon is found.
Warn'd by the wife, we fhun the baleful foil,
While down the coaft our eyes uplifted toil.

             Stupendous

Stupendous ridge! there fenc'd Seleucia lay,   120
Whence fam'd Orontes, iffuing, floods the bay.
Remov'd behind, loft Antioch mourns her fate,
For thieves a neft, and avarice a bait.
No more the bowers along the bank we trace,
Which lent to Daphne her alluring grace.   125
Murm'ring her fall, Orontes feeks the vale,
And lofty Cafius fpreads the mournful tale.
Laodicea's arms our bark invite,
Goal of her toils, and limit of her flight:
Confenting Aufter deigns her fails to court,   130
And gales propitious fpeed her to the port.

    How flits, on waking, the Enthufiaft's dream,
Who roams to realize his darling theme!
Deep-read in claffic leaves, he flights the earth,
Which giving him, ftill gave not Philip birth: 135
'Till, undeceiv'd, things take their proper hue,
And Greece, he finds, affords a Morad too.
Defcriptions foft, which caught his morning hours,
Arcadian dells, and Cytherean bow'rs,
Athenian fanes, and works immortal ftil'd,   140
Prefent but ruin, and a painful wild.

Laodicea!

Laodicea ! of a modern growth,
On whom the climate sheds the dews of sloth ;
Whose walls renown'd a worthless town infold,
As springs the weed where wav'd the ear of gold :   145
She yields him nought, his pleasing dream to save,
But some prone column or sepulchral cave :
'Till tir'd, the voyager his search gives o'er,
And, late chastis'd, prefers his native shore.

Fix'd in this maxim be my HAYLEY found,   150
To pay due homage to his native ground.
Abroad for subjects should the Druid rove,
Who draws the Muses to his haunted grove ?
Can fabled charms allure, who boasts a Fair,
The soul of grace and virtue's darling heir ?   155
Blest in his hopes, he views with pitying eye
The sweet delusions of a milder sky.
Nature herself submits to chasten'd taste,
And Eartham blooms, while Tempe lies a waste.
Mute are the lyres that charm'd th' Ægean main,   160
While Eartham's shades resound with freedom's strain.
O ! oft entreated, be that strain renew'd,
By fancy foster'd, and by praise pursu'd.

Since

Since Britain glows with liberty divine,
To rival claffic poefy be thine :   165
So fhall thy portion of the fpoils of Greece
Tranfcend the value of her golden fleece ;
As far as wit refpect o'er wealth can claim,
Or Homer foars beyond Atrides' fame !

EPISTLE

E P I S T L E III.

From COORNA, on the Conflux of the TIGRIS and EUPHRATES.

یکی دشت بیی هیه فسخ دزرد
کزان شاد کردن دل زاد مرد
هیه بیشده — — —

FERDUSI.

TRANSLATION.

" Behold yon plain, with blended colors gay,
Whose charms new rapture to the mind convey.
There gardens, groves, and rivulets abound,
And favour'd heroes confecrate the ground.
The ground like velvet feems—the rifing gale
Flings from the ftream its frefhnefs o'er the vale.
The ftalk beneath the lily's beauty bends,
The dew of fragrance on the fhade defcends.
Among the flow'rs the pheafant graceful moves,
And warbles Philomel from cyprefs groves.
Ah! from the prefent to the lateft year,
May thefe fair banks like Paradife appear!"

ARGUMENT.

Invocation.—Situation of Coorna.—Garden of Eden.—Ad-
dress to Mr. Jones the Orientalist. -Picturesque appear-
ance of the banks of the Euphrates.—-Ruins on that river
—Babylon—Anna—Circesium.—The emperor Julian.—
Palmyra.—Zenobia and Longinus.—Cities of Damascus and
Jerusalem.—Battle of Carrhæ.—Death and character of
Crassus.—The Tigris.—Retreat of the ten thousand.—Xe-
nophon.—Median wall.—Semiramis.—Cities of Seleucia
and Ctesiphon.—Origin of Bagdad, and its decline under
the Turks.—Persian authors—Pilpay—Hafez—Ferdusi.—
Transition to Britain.—Address to Liberty.—Conclusion.

E P I S T L E III.

F R O M C O O R N A,

On the Conflux of the TIGRIS and EUPHRATES.

YE Syrian mountains and Chaldean vales!
   Scenes of heroic wars and am'rous tales,
Which caught my youth, and charm'd of late mine eye,
What Mufe remifs fhall pafs your beauties by?
Immortal Genii of Obolla's ftream!   5
To HAYLEY bear a yet fublimer theme:
With orient fancy deck the clofing fong,
Rich as your banks to fpread, and as your waters ftrong.
   Plac'd on the point where Coorna rears her pride,
I mark the courfe of each defcending tide.   10

Euphrates here his limpid current pours,
While turbid Tigris deluges his fhores.
The fpace between, be antient legends true,
Where Adam firft his blufhing confort knew.
Ah feat divine! fay why thy beauties fail ?   15
Where the fweet change of thicket, hill, and dale ;
Where the clear rills that fed thy flowery plain,
Where love and innocence announce their reign ?
The fad reverfe befits our parents' crime ;
Chang'd is the face of nature, chang'd the clime :   20
The trav'ller's eye a naked champain tires,
Where pards and lions rage with ravenous fires :
T'arreft his courfe where fkulks a faithlefs race,
Fell as the prowling favage of the chace :
As if the fpot his lavifh hand array'd,   25
The vengeance of an injur'd God difplay'd !

    Ere to the ftream my vent'rous fail I give,
By which the Greek and Roman triumphs live,
Let me his Mufe invoke, whofe varied tongue
Infpirits ftill what eaftern poets fung.   30

Line 28. ' —— dum Cæfar ad altum
    Fulminat Euphratem bello.'——
                            Virg. Georg. lib. iv.

And

And while the nymphs of Iſis thee detain,
While I, unequal, try thy vivid ſtrain ;
Thou Britiſh Hafez ! prompt the magic reed,
Which hoar Euphrates to thy hand decreed.

    What novel ſcenes the verdant banks betray,   35
With ſcatter'd flocks and tented nations gay !
Illuſive fight ! which loſes ſtrait its charms ;
With paſtoral cares ill ſuits the trade of arms.
What maiden's heart can truſt the ſhepherd's ſmile,
Whoſe deeds are rapine, and whoſe words are guile ?   40
The Arab paſt—to learning what a field,
Illuſtrious Babylon ! thy ruins yield.
Devotion here with warmth ſublimer glows,
Where captive Zion breath'd melodious woes.
His impotence Ambition may be taught,   45
To view what Ammon to his ſenſes brought.
Of Glory's courſe, lo this the fatal goal !—
The victor, who could fortune's will control,
Found ruin lurking in the feſtive bowl.
But chief this ſpot the Lover's fancy feeds,   50
Where ſtill with Pyramus his Thiſbe bleeds.

Bleſt

Bleft be the chance that gave their paffion birth,
The error wept, that funk them to the earth.

Now to the weft the ftream I upward trace,
Where bord'ring culture cheers the defart fpace. 55
Lo Anna! bofom'd in her groves and ifles,
In fpite of time and gath'ring ruin, fmiles:
While loft Circefium on her chalky height
Scarce yields a veftige of her antient fite.
Thefe knew in later periods Julian's fame; 60
Ah, wherefore mark'd with an apoftate's name?
Thefe faw the hero pafs in warlike pride,
While hoftile navies fwell'd Euphrates' tide.
To conqueft pafs—but to return no more!
Him poefy, philofophy, deplore: 65
The fcepter'd patriot, who diftinctions wav'd,
Lord of himfelf, by Pagan rites enflav'd;
Whom all, but Chriftians, held their common friend,
Whofe very errors had a virtuous end:
Than Philip's fon with purer glory fir'd, 70
Expiring, to the Theban's praife afpir'd.
Leffons fevere! which home the trav'ller brings,
To waken nations, and to humble kings.

If

If yet thine eye can bear conviction's ray,
See yonder scene its mouldering pomp difplay.   75
Monarch! whate'er thy power, whate'er thy name,
No feat fuperior can thy empire claim.
Palmyra! regent of the fpacious wild,
Guardian of arts, and Freedom's younger child!
Whofe throne auguft Zenobia long pofleft,   80
Divine Longinus! in thy counfels bleft;
She, bow'd at length by Rome's refpiring force,
The brighteft trophy of Aurelian's courfe,
Still lifts her columns o'er the fubject wafte,
To chaften fculpture, and to perfect tafte.   85

Ill-fated fervant of the tuneful train!
This fcene renews their fympathetic pain.
Mid yonder fheds, while Fancy points thy grave,
Immortal tears the hallow'd fpot fhall lave.

Far to the fouth th' irriguous plain retires,   90
Whence rich Damafcus fhoots her gilded fpires.
Theme of the lover and the merchant's fong,
Where Beauty fports, and Commerce lures the throng:
Her ftreets the wealth of Hind and Ormus view,
And daily caravans the wafte renew.   95

Line 94.—" Outfhone the wealth of Ormus or of Ind."
        Milton Par. Loft, b. ii. l. 2.

With

With weightier purpose, and lefs jocund train,
The pilgrim toils to reach yon votive fane.
Him faith confirms to bear the frequent curfe,
Th' indignant blow, and taxes on his purfe :
Taxes, which Turkifh bigots term divine,   100
Who bar the Chriftian from his Saviour's fhrine.
Such the fad end of pious Frenzy's boaft,
When Europe's bigots bled on Afia's coaft :
Far different then th' imperious Chriftian came,
Glowing with monkifh zeal and promis'd fame ;   105
With claims unjuft he fann'd the raging fire,
While myriads in the mad crufade expire :
While fcenes occur, to fiction that belong,
And beft adorn the pomp of Taffo's fong.

Spread every fail, be every oar apply'd,   110
To view the triumph of barbaric pride.
Lo! where unnumber'd nations croud the plain,
And fainting cohorts fcarce the fhock fuftain.
Vers'd in thofe wiles which favage hands prepare,
The Parthian holds th' invader in the fnare.   115
In vain the veteran lifts his guardian fhield,
Rome's flaughter'd legions whiten Carrhæ's field.

And

And did no obsequies the brave await?
No column publish the Triumvir's fate?
Was History silent?—Did no partial rhimes   120
Belie his views, and varnish o'er his crimes?
A cause so venal yet demands a Muse,
And History paints him in his native hues.
Tradition says not how the robber dy'd,
Unknown th' avenging arm that crush'd his pride;   125
Yet justice found he, sacrilege to pay,
His corse, unhallow'd, sinks to dogs a prey.
To sate his avarice, the Barbarians pour
Down Crassius' throat rich streams of molten ore,
To quench a thirst, unquenchable before.   130

   A scene like this indignant let us fly,
Whose savage horrors wound the human eye;
On Fancy's pinions speed across the waste,
And Tigris' soft delights and wonders taste.
Our bark already with the current moves,   135
Here poplars bend, there breathe the citron-groves:
Aspiring cedars wave perpetual green,
And parti-color'd mosks adorn the scene.
How dead these pictures to the martial throng,
Up Tigris' banks who wound their march along;   140

                                                   O'er

O'er wilds and mountains held their toilfome way,
By hofts affaulted, and the folar ray :
By thirft, by famine, by eternal fnows—
Whom heaven and earth united to oppofe.
Unconquer'd ftill, the Greeks each peril meet,   145
Regain their fhores, and dignify retreat.
Trembling, the Mufe their daring track furveys,
And fcarce can Fancy tread the painful maze.
From red Cunaxa, ftain'd with Cyrus' blood,
They hew a paffage to the Euxine flood.   150
O'er factious bands fee eloquence prevail !
Now treaties, and now prowefs turn the fcale.
Tho' in the work ten thoufand Greeks combine,
Accomplifh'd Xenophon ! the palm is thine :
The palm, which eloquence and valor give,   155
And in thy polifh'd periods ftill fhall live.

    What tow'ring rocks the veffel's way impede,
And lift the ftream above the bord'ring mead ?
Nor Nile nor Lawrence boafts a nobler fall,
Than Tigris borrows from the Median wall ;   160
Tranfcendent labor of th' Affyrian dame !
Bold as her mind, and lafting as her fame.

                                        Seleucia

Seleucia hail !—where erft the Caliph's throne,
Fix'd by an Hermit's voice, unrivall'd fhone :
Surpaffing thee and Ctefiphon in power,   165
This Phenix fprung by mighty Nimrod's tower.
Magi of Mithra's fane ! to you I bend—
Awhile the talifmans of fable lend :
With topaz am'lets bind your Poet's arm,
That each compartment of the web may charm,   170
Where ftoried fcenes are wrought by Fairy fkill,
And Bagdad fafhion'd by Almanfor's will.

     On Tigris' banks as once the Caliph ftray'd,
His great defign by folitude to aid,
Where, proudly plac'd, might rife his royal feat,   175
Chance brought his footfteps to a fam'd retreat.
In times of yore—fo fays the Perfian tale—
A Princefs held the fceptre in the vale ;
Her flocks, the guiltlefs fubjeits of her reign,
Peace her dear wifh, and happinefs her gain.   180
Devotion's ray her tranquil bofom cheers ;
To Pagan Bagh a temple fair fhe rears ;
Where grateful vows arofe from Tigris' wave,
Whofe name a title to the valley gave.

               F   With

With changing years had chang'd the temple's lot, 185
The idol broken, and the maid forgot:
Nor yet its zealous fectaries decline,
And Mahomet adopts the Pagan fhrine.
An aged Hermit to the cell fucceeds,
Whofe hand recounts no treafure, but his beads: 190
Amid his gifts who prophecy can fum,
A mortal—confcious of events to come!
The barren court him, and the fruitful blefs,
Nor envious rumor leffens his fuccefs.

Soon as Almanfor near the temple drew,   195
The Seer his perfon and his purpofe knew.
" Hail, lord, (he cried) whofe fame the holy found,
" Be all thy projects, like the prefent, crown'd.
" Fate's hidden volume offers to mine eyes
" The favor'd fpot, where Tigris' pride fhall rife.   200
" Here fhall thy hand the Moflem Mufnud fix,
" Dreaded and potent as the throne of Styx!
" Here fhall thy tafte the Sculptor's chiffel guide,
" And Wit and Learning blend their living tide:
" Than Eden's bow'rs thy laurels greener twine,   205
" And heav'nly Houris be excell'd by thine."

He

He faid, Almanfor bows to the command,
And Bagdad's turrets awe the fubject land.

  As Sol's bright empire is a tranfient day,
Which dawns, matures, and quickly fades away,   210
The Caliph's orb revolv'd its deftin'd race,
Then vail'd in night the fplendors of its face.
It breaks again—but ah, portentous fight !
In raylefs majefty and ficken'd light.
Beneath the Othman banner Glory dies ;   215
Tafte rends her vail, and Induftry his ties :
No voice of Trade or Labor cheers the plains,
Or none but Poefy, that fings in chains.
The only veftige of declining Arts,
Some lafting tokens that the Mufe imparts ;   220
Now in the moral turn of Pilpay's ftile,
In Hafez now, on whom the Graces fmile :
Or in Ferdufi, on whofe epic ground
The lofty Homer of the Eaft is found.

  But fong avails not—nor its magic fway   225
In defolation can allure my ftay.
For climes of induftry I fpread the fail,
And Bagdad leave to deck a Fairy tale :

F 2   Leave

Leave her still miftrefs of untuneful fhades,
Unletter'd Pachas, and fecluded maids :   230
Unlike the fortune which her Tigris knows,
Who fcatters hope and plenty where he flows.

   Not that her image can the pangs renew,
From Britain's borders when thy friend withdrew.
Could man perfift when trembled Beauty's frame ?   235
Could Love endure what lovers weep to name ?
Ah ! nought that Love or Beauty could infpire,
Fond fear, wild doubt, and eloquent defire,
In Reafon's courfe could Duty's call delay,
That tore an exile from his home away.   240
To Friendfhip too his feelings ow'd a part,
And Hayley's image rufh'd upon his heart ;
Led by the Mufe who wit and tafte beguiles,
And but lefs winning than Eliza's fmiles.
Nor dumb the patriot paffion in his breaft,   245
To leave the land fo humbled and diftreft :
Her coafts alarm'd with War's terrific din,
Her councils weak, and anarchy within :
Ripe to convince th' Iberian and the Gaul,
That Britain only can by Britain fall.   250

Perifh

Perish the thought—O Liberty forefend
Thy Britain hazard the inglorious end ;
That she thro' civil broils to ruin rush,
She, whom conspiring nations fail to crush.
O ! rather give her worlds oppos'd to try,   255
Combin'd to conquer, or combin'd to die :
With thee, bright Goddess ! to renown aspire,
In life possess thee, or in death acquire !

N O T E S.

N O T E S

ON THE

F I R S T   E P I S T L E.

LINE 4. " ―――― which ADDISON *defign'd*."

Alluding to the fketch which he has given us of Venice, in the elegant and claffical travels under his name.

Line 16. " ―――― *and where Paulo taught*."

The merit of Paul Calliari, called the Veronefe, need not be defcanted on here; but to the curious anecdotes which Mr. Hayley has given us of the feveral mafters, in the notes of his Epiftle to an Eminent Painter, I beg leave to add one, which I picked up at Venice. On the records of the monaftery of St. Georgio Maggiori it appears, that the Monks gave Paul Veronefe but 100 livres, and a butt of wine of 30 livres more, making together about 3 *l.* fterling, for his admirable picture of the Marriage of Cana, which hangs up in their refectory. This piece is of an amazing fize, and not only contains above a hundred figures as big as life, but among the guefts the painter has introduced the principal monarchs and perfonages of his age, not omitting Titian and himfelf. But this fpeaks lefs for its value than the propofal of Lewis XIV. (which has been fince applied falfely to other good paintings) who offered to cover the picture with louifdores; and if that was infufficient, to double the fum. Whether the price fell fhort of its worth, or be-

G
ing

ing public property, it could not be difposed of, the king was difap-
pointed. A natural inference however will be drawn from the
circumstance, and the prefent value of the piece be greatly hcight-
ened, which in the laft age was held in fuch eftimation. The original coft of the picture, and its after fortune, remind us of the
fate of Milton's Paradife Loft, which, under-valued and over-
looked during the author's life, has alone infured him immortality,
and is become the ornament of literature, and the delight of mankind. Paul Calliari has a monument and infcription in the church
of St. Sebaftian, which is almoft wholly decorated with his paintings.

Line 18. " *Where proud Ca' Dona overhangs the lake.*"

The name of a palace on the Fondamento Nuovo. This noble
terrace lines the north-weft afpect of Venice; is much reforted to
in fummer by the inhabitants, and commands the beautiful view
which the Poem defcribes.

Line 42. " *And bind the lover an eternal flave.*"

This farcafm is founded on the cuftom which the Venetian ladies
have eftablifhed of entertaining a cavaliero fervanto. The ties of
this enamorato are not lefs binding than thofe of matrimony. His
mornings and evenings, at leaft, muft be fpent in attendance on his
fair-one; nor can he be feen in a public place in company with
another woman. The obligation, it is true, holds equally on her
fide; fo that they may be faid to purchafe dearly the illicit plea-
fures which cuftom allows them.

Line 49. " *And hoftile rumors, that from Auftria fly.*"

The weaknefs of the Venetian ftate, and the known difpofition
of a very powerful and encroaching neighbor, feem to portend
fome unfavorable change, which the powers of Europe may be too
much engaged to prevent.

Line 62.

Line 62. *" Thine iflands cherifh'd Rome's expiring band."*

If tradition does not immediately trace the connexion between the two Republics, circumftances manifeftly fuggeft the probability of the fact. It is recorded that a people called the Veniti, dwelling about Padua and the river Po, were obliged, in the fifth century, by the ravages of the barbarian Attila, to take refuge among the cluſter of ſmall iflands at the head of the Adriatic gulf. From the huts of fifhermen, and the little barks that earned them a livelihood, have arifen the ftately palaces, and unbounded commerce of the city of Venice. But fome authors derive her origin from the Franks, and fome from the Henetians, a nation bordering on Paphlagonia.

POLYBIUS. CORN. NEP. LIVY. SANSOV.

Line 67. *" Great as Æmilius, in that hallow'd hour."*

In allufion to that celebrated day on which the Roman Proconful, P. Æmilius, proclaimed the freedom of Greece to the nations affembled at the Olympic games.

Line 76. *" And Morofini in his art furvives!"*

Francifco Morofini, the General and afterwards Doge of Venice. His defence of Candia rendered his name immortal. He conquered the Morea from the Turks, A. D. 1683, and had the honor to have his actions recorded by the pencils of Palma, Titian, &c. in the palace of St. Marco.

Line 81. *Arizzo, glorying in a cruel death."*

Paolo Arizzo, one of the Venetian generals in their wars with the Turks. He was taken prifoner in Negropont by the Sultan Mahomet II, and condemned to be placed between two boards, and fawn afunder alive, by the faithlefs barbarity of that tyrant; who

G 2

having

having promifed to fpare his head, excufed himfelf by faying, the trunk was not included.

Line 84.   " *Still brave Antonio may his fate defy.*"

Marco Antonio Bragadino, the gallant defender of the city of Famagoufta againft the whole force of the Ottoman empire, during the memorable fiege wherein the Turks are faid to have loft one hundred thoufand men. He was obliged at length by famine to furrender, in A. D. 1571, and obtained the honorable conditions that his defence merited; but the Pacha Muftapha, in a perfidious manner, broke the capitulation, and vented his inhuman revenge on the brave Bragadino. He was firft put to the moft excruciating tortures, and then flayed alive by the tyrant's order, and his fkin ftuffed with ftraw, and fufpended on the maft-head of the admiral's galley. With this inglorious trophy he returned to Conftantinople, and fullied even the parade of victory. A baffo-relievo of the ftories of Arizzo and Bragadino is to be found in the arfenal of Venice; and in the church of St. Gio and Paolo, the fkin of Bragadino is enclofed in a marble urn, with his ftatue in marble above it. There is alfo a monument to that hero in the church of St. Gregorio.

PARUTA. MORISINI.

Line 95.   " *Envy to calm, fhe trufted to intrigue,*
            And, artful, broke the force of Cambray's league."

This confederacy, which threatened the very exiftence of the Venetian ftate, is known to Europe under the name of the league of Cambray. The Emperor Maximilian, Lewis XII, and Ferdinand of Arragon, were the heads of this confpiracy, which was engendered and fupported by the artifices of Pope Julius II. Several of the neighboring Italian ftates feceded to the league; and nothing could have faved the Republic from deftruction, but her finding

means

means to buy off the Pope, by an artful application to the resentment, pride, and avarice of the ambitious Pontiff.

BEMBO. BARRE. GUICCIARD. SANSOV.

Line 106. " —— or San Benetto stood."

The theatre where the serious opera is performed during the Carnival.

Line 113. " Deck'd with the spoils of many a falling pile,
That erst o'erlook'd the Bosphorus or Nile."

The traveller who has visited Venice will enter into this couplet. The stately Gothic church of St. Marco is a composition of marbles, drawn from every place where the Venetians were victorious. Nor was their plunder reserved for the use of their churches. The lions at the gate of the arsenal were brought from the port of Athens, named therefrom; the granite pillars on the place of St. Marco, from Alexandria; and the inimitable brazen horses over the door of St. Marco's church, from Constantinople, at the different periods that these cities were in the hands of the Venetians.

Line 118. " And with Lysippus class a Sansovin."

Iachimo Sanfovino, a celebrated architect and sculptor, who lived in the sixteenth century. His chef d'œuvres in basso relievo adorn the ducal church of St. Marco; and as an architect, the Public Library, the Lodge opposite the gate of the ducal palace, the New Palace on the place of St. Marco, the Scuola della Misericordia, and the churches of St. Francisco della Vigna and St. Geminiano, speak more for his excellence than the pen can do. He was buried in the latter church, which would sufficiently record his memory; but his son Francisco Sanfovino, the author of the History of Venice, the Origin of the Illustrious Houses of Italy, and other esteemed tracts, has inscribed an epitaph to his renowned parent.

parent. Above the epitaph is the ſtatue of the architect, cut by himſelf; and facing it, that of the hiſtorian, his ſon.

Line 125. *" Deriv'd new lights from learn'd Farſetti's toil."*

The collection here alluded to, is perhaps the nobleſt in the poſſeſſion of any ſubject in any ſtate. The ingenious nobleman, now deceaſed, foreſeeing the difficulty of procuring originals, at great pains and expence employed the firſt artiſts of his age, to furniſh him with caſts of the moſt valuable remains of antiquity. Whatever, therefore, excites the attention of taſte and learning, whatever Rome or Florence can boaſt of, is to be found in this muſeum; which, to the credit of the preſent proprietor, is always eaſy of acceſs, and particularly to a foreigner. What the agreeable Dr. Moore relates of Prince Ferdinand of Brunſwick, in his Travels, is ſomewhat ſimilar to this purſuit. The Prince not being in circumſtances to purchaſe original paintings, wiſely determined to be maſter of what he could compaſs, and has accordingly furniſhed his palace with the beſt prints of the beſt maſters.

Line 127. *" Once more a village—Venice all deplore."*

Caſſiodorus, ſpeaking of the Venetians, about fifty years after their foundation, ſays, that they inhabited the iſlands of the Adriatic: that they had no other fence againſt the waves but hurdles; no other food but fiſh; no wealth beſides their boats; and no merchandiſe but ſalt.

CASSIOD. b. xii. ep. 24.

NOTES

N O T E S

ON THE

SECOND EPISTLE.

LINE 11. " *Thine ifle, Corcyra, next attracts our view.*"
Hod. Corfu.——PLINY, b. iv. c. 11.

Line 18. " *Where Corinth reign'd the fovereign of the waves.*"

This city was formerly much reforted to, on account of its havens towards the Ionian and Ægean feas; whence Ovid calls it " Bimarem Corinthon." Met. v. 407.

Line 21. " *Alpheus now, without a fiction, glides.*"

This river was fabled to have funk underground near Pifa in Greece, and running through the fea without mingling its waters, to have rifen with the fountain Arethufa in Syracufe, in Sicily. It falls into the Ionian fea.
VIRG. Æn. b. iii. l. 694. Ov. Amor. iii. 6.

Line 23. " *And anxious double bleak Methone's ftrand.*"
Hod. Cape Modon.——VAL. FLACC. b. i. l. 388.

Line 30. " *And now we gaze on Cytherea's ifle.*"
Hod. Cerigo. —— VIRG. Æn. b. x. l. 51.

Line

Line 41.   " *In Lerna's fen, or Pholoe's savage height.*"

Veteri fpumavit Lerna veneno.   STAT. Theb. b. i. l. 360.
— et populum Pholoe mentita biformem.
                               LUC. lib. iii. ver. 198.

Line 56.   " *Thus fighs the Mufe in paffing Milo's coaft.*"
                 Olim Melos.

Line 57.   " *And Nio, proud of Homer's urn to boaft.*"

Olim Ios—an ifland in the Myrtean fea, where Homer was en-
tombed.   PLIN. b. iv. c. 12.

Line 58.   " *Serphos, on which the fabled fcene is laid.*"

Olim Seriphos—a fmall ifland where Polydutus reigned; whofe
fair daughter was the reward of Perfeus' heroifm. Thus fays the
fable. Origen, fpeaking of this ifland, terms it " Minima & ig-
nobiliffima infula."

Line 60.   " *Paros, whofe marble gave the ifle to fame.*"

Paros, marmore nobilis.   PLIN. Hift. Nat. b. iv. c. 12.

Line 61.   " *And Naxos, whence the God of vintage came.*"

Bacchata jugis Naxos.   VIRG. Æn. b. iv. l. 125.

Line 63.   *Where Med'cine's pride arofe, and Painting's laft.*"

Hod. Stanchio—the native ifle of Hippocrates and Apelles.

Line 83.   " *Next, fallen Cyprus! gives us fight of thee.*"
                         VIRG. Æn. b. i. l. 126. HOR. Od. i. 19.
                                                    Line

Line 96. " *Majestic Lebanon his head uprears.*"

Line 98. " *Tho' fall'n his pride, some cedars yet remain.*"

" The inhabitants of Lebanon hold these cedars in such veneration, on account of their having been recorded by David and Solomon, that they will not suffer the six or seven remaining old trees to be destroyed." Man. Tour of the Rev. JOHN HUSSEY.

Line 104. " *Those walls, which turn'd young Ammon's conqu'ring*
 sword." Q. CUR. iv.—4. 19.

Line 107. " *Can scarcely shield the fisher from his fate !*"

" And they shall destroy the walls of Tyrus, and break down her towers : I will also scrape her dust from her, and make her like the top of a rock.

It shall be a place for the spreading of nets in the midst of the sea." EZEKIEL xxvi. 4, 5.

Line 108. " *Not so when Dido fled thy hostile strand.*"
 JUST. xviii. 6.

Line 117. " *Where moist, unpeopled Scanderoon is found.*"

Also called Alexandretta. Olim Alexandria.

Line 120. " *Stupendous ridge ! there, fenc'd, Seleucia lay.*"
 Seleucia Pieria.——PLIN. V. 21.

Line 121. " *Whence fam'd Orontes, issuing, floods the bay.*"
 Hod. Asti.——Ov. Met. b. ii. l. 248.

Line 122. " *Remov'd behind, lost Antioch mourns her fate.*"
 PLIN. V. 12.

It is remarked that the disciples of our Lord were first called Christians at Antioch.

Line 124.   " *No more the bowers along the bank we trace,*
            Which lent to Daphne her alluring grace."

The charms of this retreat were such, as to occasion the proverb,
" Daphnicis moribus vivere."   EUTROP. vi. 11.
                    " Nor that fweet grove,
Of Daphne by Orontes."   MILTON Par. Loft, b. iv. l. 273.

Line 127.   " *And lofty Cofius fpreads the mournful tale.*"
                                PLIN. v. 22.

Line 128.   " *Laodicea's arms our bark invite.*"——Hod. Latichea.

The catacombs in this neighborhood are as grand and perfect as
any remains of that kind now extant.
                                CIC. Philip. ix. 2.

Line 137.   " *And Greece, he finds, affords a Morad too.*"

The Sultan Morad IV. whofe abominable vices were yet gloffed
over by the extraordinary endowments of his perfon and mind. His
levity and impetuofity gave birth to numerous adventures, which
the Turks are fond of blending with the marvellous in their ac-
counts of this uncommon perfonage. But his horrid cruelties feem
chiefly to have originated from his frequent inebriety; and a ftory
which they relate of him at the fiege of Bagdad, is perhaps as
pofitive a teftimony of the power of mufic, as hiftory or fable can
produce. It is thus tranflated from the Ottoman hiftorian, Prince
Cantemir:
    " The Perfians ftill mourn the cruelty of Morad, who directed
that no captive fhould be fpared when Bagdad was ftormed. One
perfon, when the officers were going to kill him, defired that he
might fpeak a word to the Sultan before his death. Being brought
before him, and afked what he had to fay: " Suffer not (he cried)
" moft gracious emperor, that with me, Sheh Kuli, the whole art
" of mufic fhould perifh." Being ordered to give a fpecimen of
                                                            his

his skill, he takes up a Shechdar (called in Arabic Zabur, and in
Greek Pfalterio) and with so much art as well as sweetness, both
played and sung the tragedy of the taking of Bagdad, intermixed
with Morad's praises, that the Soltan could not refrain from tears
all the while he was performing.   For this musician's sake, Morad
set at liberty all who had not been yet massacred ; and his musical
works became famous in Turkey."   This instrument is much like
an harp, with six strings each way, as the word Shechdar denotes.
It is said to have been invented by David ; though few at present
know how to play well on it.

Mod. Un. Hist. vol. xii. b. xv. c. 18.

N O T E S

ON THE

THIRD EPISTLE.

LINE 5. " *Immortal Genii of Obolla's stream!*"

Commonly called the Shut Ul Arab, or great river of the Arabs. This was the Pafitigris of the antients, and the Obolla of the Perfian poets. JONES's Defcrip. of Afia.

Line 9. " *Plac'd on the point where Coorna rears her pride.*"

Olim Apamea—a city built on the conflux of the rivers. Its fituation is ftrong, but quite neglected by the Turks.
D'ANVILLE.

Line 13. " *The fpace between, be antient legends true,*
Where Adam firft his blufhing confort knew."

The authority of Milton may render this notion indifputable. It were needlefs to offer evidence in fupport of his learned page.

" Eden ftretch'd her line
From Auran eaftward to the royal towers
Of great Seleucia." Par. Loft, b. iv. l. 210.
" There was a place
Where Tigris at the foot of Paradife." B. ix. l. 71.

Line

Line 33. " *Thou British Hafez! prompt the magic reed.*"

The reader will not be at a loss to fix on the person thus characterized. The ingenious specimens which Mr. Jones has given of Eastern poetry, must make the public regret that other pursuits have put a stop to his prosecuting his discoveries on the remoter shores of literature.

Line 42. " *Illustrious Babylon! thy ruins yield.*"

The ruins of Babylon are yet pointed out by the Arab on the eastern bank of the Euphrates, nearly opposite the present town of Hilla; but these ruins are probably more modern, though built on the site of the antient city. STRAB. p. 738.

Line 44. " *Where captive Zion breath'd melodious woes.*"

" By the waters of Babylon we sat down and wept, when we remembered thee, O Sion." Psalm cxxxvii.

Line 56. " *Lo Anna! bosom'd in her groves and isles.*"

Olim Anatho.—It is worthy of remark, that there is little change in the appearance or government of this place, since it was visited by the Emperor Julian, above 1,400 years ago. It is built on each side of the Euphrates, and on an island in the middle of the stream, and still in the hands of an Arabian Emir, under the Pacha of Bagdad.

Line 58. " *While lost Circesium on her chalky height.*"

A frontier town of the Roman empire, situated on the conflux of the Araxes and Euphrates; and mentioned in this light in the treaty of peace concluded by Diocletian with the Persian King Narses. PROCOP. b. x.

Line 60.   " *Thefe knew in later periods Julian's fame.*"

Line 71.   " *Expiring, to the Theban's praife efpir'd.*"

The defection of this great man from the pureft of all religions,
cannot be defended, though it may be accounted for; and his aver-
fion and difcountenance to Chriftians, fuits not the informed and
liberal mind of Julian in other points.   It will fuffice to fay, that
his life feems to have belied the name of Apoftate, which he brought
upon himfelf by his deviation from the faith he was educated in.
If the paths of Virtue lead to the temple of Truth, he invariably
trod them; and may charitably be fuppofed to have arrived, by an
indirect courfe, at the divine goal.   The circumftances of his death
are fo fimilar to thofe of Epaminondas, that we muft be rejoiced to
find their lives were equally dignified by purfuits that rendered
their end immortal.

AMMIAN. b. xvi. p. 62.   LIBAN. Orat. xii. p. 288.

Line 78.   " *Palmyra! regent of the fpacious wild.*"

Line 80.   " *Whofe throne auguft Zenobia long poffeft.*"

This queen is one of the moft illuftrious women mentioned in
hiftory.   She derived her pedigree from the Ptolomies of Egypt;
was well verfed in all the branches of polite literature; underftood
thoroughly the Egyptian, Greek, and Latin languages; and in the
knowledge of hiftory, excelled moft men of her time.   She had
great fhare in the victories gained by her hufband Odenatus over
the Perfians, and is faid to have been no lefs courageous than that
brave commander, and equally experienced in military affairs.

AUR. Vit. p. 219.   Ant. Un. Hift. vol. xv. c. 24.

Line 84.   " *Still lifts her columns o'er the fubject wafte,*
              To chafton Sculpture, and to perfect Tafte."

The world are indebted to the ingenious travellers, Meffrs. Wood
and Dawkins, for the elegant remains of Palmyra.   What was her
                                                        fituation

fituation in the days of her profperity, may be gathered from the
following defcription:

" Such were once the magnificent abodes, and fuch the noble
fepulchres of the Palmyrenians. From what we have faid of both,
we may well conclude, that the world never faw a more glorious
city. A city, not more remarkable for its ftately buildings, than for
the extraordinary perfonages who once flourifhed in it; among
whom the renowned Zenobia, and the incomparable Longinus,
muft for ever be remembered with admiration and regret."

Ant. Un. Hift. vol. ii. c. 5.   Wood's Jour. to Palmyra.

The deportment of Zenobia after fhe became a prifoner, was
quite inconfiftent with her former magnanimity, and in fome de-
gree fullied the brightnefs of her character. The love of life
adhered fo clofely to her, when all which rendered it of value was
gone, that fhe was induced to give up her fecretary, Longinus, as
the author and advifer of the remarkable letter, which provoked the
emperor's refentment during the fiege of Palmyra. The revenge
which Aurelian took on this occafion was ftill meaner, and more
difgraceful than her treachery.   Zosimus, l. i. p. 51.

Line 97. " *The pilgrim toils to reach yon votive fane.*"

The hardfhips and dangers of a pilgrimage to Jerufalem, have
been defcribed by fo many travellers, that the author need not add
any particulars that have occurred within his knowledge, to confirm
them. The injuftice of the motives, and the ill confequences
which have attended the Crufades, come too home to be difputed
by the prefent race of Chriftians in Paleftine.   Sandys.

Line 117. " *Rome's flaughter'd legions whiten Carrhæ's field.*"

This battle is called by the Latin authors, the battle of Carrhæ,
becaufe it was fought at a fmall diftance from that city. It was,
without difpute, the moft terrible blow, after the battle of Cannæ,
which the Romans ever received.

Ant. Un. Hift. vol. ii. c. 12.   Eutrop. l. vi.

Line 124.   *" Tradition says not how the robber dy'd."*

Writers leave it in doubt whether Craffus was killed by his own men, to prevent his falling alive into the enemy's hands, or by the Parthians.   Liv. l. cvi.   Flor. b. iii. c. 2.

Line 126.   *" Yet justice found he, sacrilege to pay,*
             His corse unhallow'd."

The plundering the temple of Jerusalem was not the only sacrilege that Craffus was guilty of. He robbed, in like manner, all the temples of Syria, appropriating to his own use their rich ornaments and furniture. The temple of the Syrian goddess, named Atargetis, at Hieropolis, which some writers call Bambyces, others Edeffa, and the Syrians Magog, was famous all over the East, on account of the immense treasures laid up there, as being the collection of many years. These the avaricious Proconful feized; and, left any of the rich vases and ornaments fhould be embezzled, he fpent a great deal of his time in feeing the money counted, and the gold and filver veffels weighed before him. In fhort, there was not any means of amaffing money, how unjuft and oppreffive foever, which he did not ufe; as if he had been fent, not to govern but plunder the provinces. Ant. Un. Hift. vol. ii. c. 12. Strabo, b. xvi. p. 748.   Plin. b. v. c. 23.

Line 129.   *" Down Craffus' throat rich ftreams of molten ore."*
                         Flor. b. iii. c. 2.   Dio. Cass. b. xi.

Line 139.   *" How dead thofe pictures to the mortal throng,*
             Up Tigris' banks who wound their march along."

Line 153.   *" Tho' in the work ten thoufand Greeks combine,*
             Accomplifh'd Xenophon! the palm is thine."

The retreat of the ten thoufand Greeks, is a tranfaction too celebrated in hiftory to be unknown to the reader; but it may not
                                                                              be

be unuseful to bring the outlines into one point of view, to recall the value of the picture to his memory.

This retreat was a march of 2,325 miles, the longest we read of in history, through the territories of a powerful and victorious enemy, and under all imaginable dangers and difficulties. It is fortunate for the world, that a long and memorable series of exploits, achieved by an army of 10,000 men, and under the conduct of one of the wisest and completest generals of antiquity, has been transmitted to posterity by his own inimitable pen.

After the battle of Cunaxa, and the death of Cyrus, in whose behalf the Greeks had engaged in the expedition against Artaxerxes, their camp was plundered, themselves in a victorious enemy's country, and at a vast distance from their own, and every moment expecting to feel the severest effects of the king's resentment. It was in this extreme difficulty that Xenophon began to give those signal proofs of his bravery, sagacity, and eloquence, by which he not only inspired the desponding Greeks with fresh courage, but persuaded their remaining chiefs to resolve on this noble, though arduous and dangerous retreat; and, after the death of Clearchus, to appoint him their general. What still enhances his merit on this occasion is, that he had never borne any command or commission before; and was, as is commonly supposed, under thirty years of age when he was raised to that dignity.

From Cunaxa the Greeks retreated through the Median wall to Sitace. Here they passed the Tigris by a bridge of boats, and coasted that river for some time. Their route lay through Seleucia (now Bagdad) and the Median deserts, to Coene. Here they crossed the Zabatus, which falls into the Tigris, and arrived at Mespila, where they determined to quit the river, and force their way over the Carduchian mountains. Continually harrassed by the enemy, and stripped of their baggage, the Greeks at length gained the head of the Euphrates. Hence they continued their course to the Araxes, and passing through the territories of the Chalybeans, or Georgians, came to Colchis, on the Euxine sea. We shall here

I   leave

leave them, as they have arrived at the goal which they had fo ardently panted for, and now began to feparate, and to purfue their way homewards by different routes.

Ant. Un. Hift. vol. vii. b. ii. Xenoph. Diod. Sic.

Line 159.   " *Nor Nile nor Lawrence boafts a nobler fall,*
            Than Tigris borrows from the Median wall."

The river St. Lawrence in North America, which contains the ftupendous cataract of Niagara.   As to the wall of Semiramis, defcribed in hiftory as running from the Euphrates to the Tigris, there are at prefent no traces of it, except the maffive mafonry which croffes the Tigris at Tekrid, and interrupts the navigation of the river, can be confidered as a fragment of that noble work.   The folidity of this mafonry, its fituation, and apparent obftruction to the channel, feem to countenance a conjecture, which cannot be decided by the imperfect annals of the country.   The Tigris above Bagdad is navigated by a raft, formed of reeds, and buoyed up by bladders.   When this raft arrives at Tekrid, the mariners take it out of the water, and launch it again below the wall; which could not be done with a lefs fimple veffel of equal fize, unattended with confiderable trouble and expence.

Line 163.   " *Seleucia hail!—where erft the Caliph's throne.*"

———

Line 165.   " *Surpaffing thee and Ctefiphon in power,*
            This Phenix fprung by mighty Nimrod's tower."

The general opinion that Bagdad is built near the fpot where Seleucia and Ctefiphon formerly ftood, is adopted by hiftorians and modern travellers.   A lofty and antient tower, which ftands in the plain to the weftward of Bagdad, and ferved as a land-mark to us, is commonly known by the name of Nimrod's Tower.

Mod. Un. Hift. vol. ii. c. 2.   Ives's Voyages.

9

Line 173. " *On Tigris' banks as once the Caliph stray'd,*
               His great design."

The story of the Caliph Almansor, or, in Arabic, Al Mansur, re-
lative to the building of Bagdad, is told nearly in the same manner
by different writers. Though the Orientals are fond of introdu-
cing the marvellous even into their hiftorical page, and this tale of
the Hermit is agreeable to their fuperftitious turn, it might have
happened in a more enlightened age and country.

GREG. Abul. Farai. Geograph. Perf. apud D'HERBEL.
Biblioth. Orient. in art. Bagd.

Line 193. " *The barren court him, and the fruitful blefs.*"

This picture of a Mahometan Santo will not appear forced or
unnatural to thofe who have read the Travels of Tournefort, Nie-
buhr, &c. But a more ftriking anecdote than I have elfewhere
met with of thefe impoftors, was related to me at Aleppo, as having fallen within the knowledge of the prefent Britifh conful.

A naked Santo came one day to the door of a merchant of Aleppo.
His bufinefs was to demand charity; but the miftrefs of the houfe
obferving him through a window, took the occafion of her hufband's
abfence to beckon him to enter her apartment. Accuftomed to
thefe invitations, he was not flow in obeying the fign, and in fatif-
fying the amorous defires of the lady. He retired from the confe-
rence without fufpicion; but fuch were the uncommon attractions
of the fair ftranger, that he returned the next day to partake of
the forbidden banquet. He knocked boldly at the gate; but, as
chance directed, it was opened by the hufband, whofe perfon was
known to him. There was now no refource but in the fuper-
ftition of the Turks; and with the effrontery that marks his fect,
he afked the merchant for his wife! The novelty of the queftion
in the Eaft, the character of thefe religious, and the difturbed ftate
into which his paffions had thrown him, all confpired to favor the
Santo's defigns. A ftrange whim immediately poffeft the merchant.
He

He perfuaded himfelf that the Santo had been infpired to demand his wife ; and, like a good Muffulman, holding it impious to refift the decrees of fate, he readily fought the lady to difpofe her for the vifit. This, it feems, proved a lefs difficult tafk than his fimplicity had apprehended. The honeft man brought them together, and while the happy pair were laughing at his credulity, he was bleffing himfelf for the favorable compliance of his wife, and feeding his imagination with the probable iffue of an embrace that had been fanctified by the Prophet.

Line 201.   " *Here fhall thy hand the Meflem Mufund—*"

The Oriental appellation for a throne.

Line 211.   " *The Caliph's orb revolv'd its deflin'd race.*"

Line 213.   " *It breaks again.*"

Line 215.   " *Beneath the Othman banner Glory dies.*"

The deftruction of the Caliphate by the Turks, forms a memorable æra in hiflory. The vifible decline of arts, induftry, and population, throughout the Grand Signior's dominions, is the melancholy reflexion of every traveller.

TOURNEFORT. POCOCKE. CHANDLER.

Line 221.   " *Now in the moral turn of Pilpay's flile,*
                 In Hafez now, on whom the Graces fmile :
                 Or in Ferdufi."

The curious reader may find a full account of the various works and merits of thefe Poets, in an hiflory of the Perfian language, annexed by the learned Mr. Jones to his Life of Nader Shaw. From this fource the motto to this Epiftle was taken, the original poem being very fcarce in India.

F I N I S.

www.ingramcontent.com/pod-product-compliance
Lightning Source LLC
Chambersburg PA
CBHW022029080426
42733CB00007B/772